BULLETPOINTS

WEATHER & CLIMATE

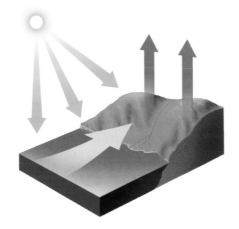

John Farndon
Consultant: Peter Riley

Miles Kelly
PUBLISHING

First published by Miles Kelly Publishing Ltd
Bardfield Centre, Great Bardfield
Essex, CM7 4SL

2 4 6 8 10 9 7 5 3 1

Editor
Isla MacCuish

Design
WhiteLight

Picture Research
Liberty Newton

Inputting
Carol Danenbergs

British Library Cataloguing-in-Publication Data
A catalogue record for this book is available from the British Library

ISBN 1-84236-239-9

Printed in China

www.mileskelly.net
info@mileskelly.net

The publishers would like to thank the following artists who have contributed to this book:

Gary Hincks, Janos Marffy, Guy Smith

Contents

Climate

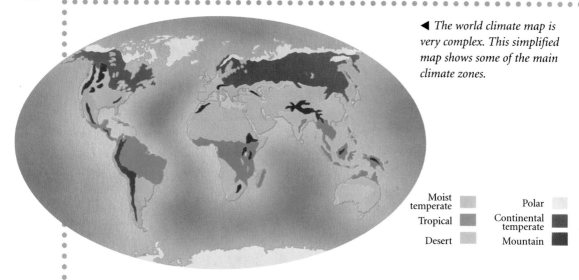

◀ *The world climate map is very complex. This simplified map shows some of the main climate zones.*

Moist temperate

Tropical

Desert

Polar

Continental temperate

Mountain

- **Climate is the typical weather** of a place over a long time.
- **Climates are warm** near the Equator, where the Sun climbs high in the sky.
- **Tropical climates** are warm climates in the tropical zones on either side of the Equator. Average temperatures of 27°C are typical.
- **The climate is cool** near the Poles, where the Sun never climbs high in the sky. Average temperatures of −30°C are typical.
- **Temperate climates** are mild climates in the temperate zones between the tropics and the polar regions. Summer temperatures may average 23°C. Winter temperatures may average 12°C.
- **A Mediterranean climate** is a temperate climate with warm summers and mild winters. It is typical of the Mediterranean, California, South Africa and South Australia.

▶ *The big seasonal difference in temperature is due to the movement of the overhead Sun. The polar regions are too far away from the Equator for the Sun ever to be overhead, or for there to be much seasonal difference in temperature.*

▶ *When the Mediterranean is nearest the Sun in midsummer it is hottest and driest. The coolest time of year comes when the Sun is farthest away from the Mediterranean, and closer to the southern hemisphere.*

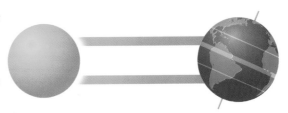

▶ *There is little seasonal variation in temperature near the Equator. Moving away from the Equator, there are seasons. The Sun is directly above the Equator during March and September, and above the Tropics of Cancer and Capricorn in June and December.*

- **A monsoon climate** is a climate with one very wet and one very dry season – typical of India and SE Asia.

- **An oceanic climate** is a wetter climate near oceans, with cooler summers and warmer winters.

- **A continental climate** is a drier climate in the centre of continents, with hot summers and cold winters.

- **Mountain climates** get colder and windier with height.

Climate change

▲ *Tree rings can be used to tell what the weather has been like in the past. In wet periods the rings are thick and in dry periods the rings are thin.*

- **The world's climate** is changing all the time, getting warmer, colder, wetter or drier. There are many theories why this happens.

- **One way to see** how climate changed before weather records were kept is to look at the growth rings in old trees.

- **Another way** of working out past climate is to look in ancient sediments for remains of plants and animals that only thrive in certain conditions.

- **One cause of climate change** may be shifts in the Earth's orientation to the Sun. These shifts are called Milankovitch cycles.

- **One Milankovitch cycle** is the way the Earth's axis wobbles round like a top every 21,000 years. Another is the way its axis tilts like a rolling ship every 40,000 years. A third is the way its orbit gets more or less oval shaped every 96,000 years.

- **Climate** may also be affected by dark patches on the Sun called sunspots. These flare up and down every 11 years.

- **Sunspot activity** is linked to stormy weather on the Earth.

- **Climates may cool** when the air is filled with dust from volcanic eruptions or meteors hitting the Earth.

- **Climates** may get warmer when levels of certain gases in the air increase (see global warming).

- **Local climates** may change as continents drift around. Antarctica was once in the tropics, while the New York area once had a tropical desert climate.

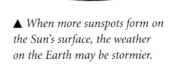

▲ *When more sunspots form on the Sun's surface, the weather on the Earth may be stormier.*

7

Atmosphere

- **The atmosphere** is a blanket of gases about 1000 km deep around the Earth. It can be divided into five layers: troposphere (the lowest), stratosphere, mesosphere, thermosphere and exosphere.

- **The atmosphere** is: 78% nitrogen, 21% oxygen, 1% argon and carbon dioxide with tiny traces of neon, krypton, zenon, helium, nitrous oxide, methane and carbon monoxide.

- **The atmosphere** was first created by the fumes pouring out from the volcanoes that covered the early Earth 4000 million years ago. But it was changed as rocks and seawater absorbed carbon dioxide, and then algae in the sea built up oxygen levels over millions and millions of years.

- **The troposphere** is just 12 km thick yet it contains 75% of the weight of gases in the atmosphere. Temperatures drop with height from 18°C on average to about –60°C at the top, called the tropopause.

- **The stratosphere** contains little water. Unlike the troposphere, which is heated from below, it is heated from above as the ozone in it is heated by ultraviolet light from the Sun. Temperatures rise with height from –60°C to 10°C at the top, about 50 km up.

- **The stratosphere** is completely clear and calm, which is why jet airliners try to fly in this layer.

- **The mesosphere** contains few gases but it is thick enough to slow down meteorites. They burn up as they hurtle into it, leaving fiery trails in the night sky. Temperatures drop from 10°C to –120°C 80 km up.

> **...FASCINATING FACT...**
> The stratosphere glows faintly at night because sodium from salty sea spray reacts chemically in the air.

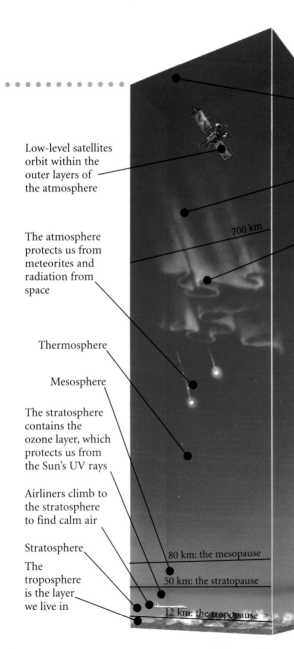

Light gases such as hydrogen and helium continually drift into space from the outer fringes of the atmosphere

Low-level satellites orbit within the outer layers of the atmosphere

Exosphere

The atmosphere protects us from meteorites and radiation from space

Shimmering curtains of light called auroras appear above the poles. They are caused by the impact of particles from the Sun on the gases in the upper atmosphere

700 km

Thermosphere

- **In the thermosphere** temperatures are very high, but there is so little gas that there is little real heat. Temperatures rise from −120°C to 2000°C 700 km up.

Mesosphere

The stratosphere contains the ozone layer, which protects us from the Sun's UV rays

- **The exosphere** is the highest level of the atmosphere where it fades into the nothingness of space.

Airliners climb to the stratosphere to find calm air

Stratosphere

The troposphere is the layer we live in

80 km: the mesopause

50 km: the stratopause

12 km: the tropopause

◀ The atmosphere is a sea of colourless, tasteless, odourless gases, mixed with moisture and fine dust particles. It is about 1000 km deep but has no distinct edge, simply fading away into space. As you move up, each layer contains less and less gas. The topmost layers are very rarefied, which means that gas is very sparse.

9

Clouds

Cumulonimbus thunder clouds are the
tallest clouds, often over 10 km high.

▲ *Cirrus clouds appear high in the sky, sometimes at heights of over 10,000 m.*

● **Clouds are** dense masses of water drops and ice crystals that are so tiny they
float high in the air.

● **Cumulus clouds** are fluffy white clouds. They pile up as warm air rises and
cool to the point where water vapour condenses.

● **Strong updraughts** create huge cumulonimbus, or thunder, clouds.

▶ *Cumulus clouds build up in fluffy piles as warm, moist air rises. Once it reaches about 2000 m, the air cools enough for clouds to form.*

- **Stratus clouds** are vast shapeless clouds that form when a layer of air cools to the point where moisture condenses. They often bring long periods of light rain.

- **Cirrus clouds** are wispy clouds that form so high up they are made entirely of ice. Strong winds high up blow them into 'mares tails'.

- **Low clouds** lie below 2000 m above the ground. They include stratus and stratocumulus clouds (the spread tops of cumulus clouds).

- **Middle clouds** often have the prefix 'alto' and lie from 2000 m to 6000 m up. They include rolls of altocumulus cloud, and thin sheets called altostratus.

- **High-level clouds** are ice clouds up to 11,000 m up. They include cirrus, cirrostratus and cirrocumulus.

- **Contrails** are trails of ice crystals left by jet aircraft.

Fog and mist

▲ *Fog spreads slowly upwards from the surface of the water seen here over the Ganges in India.*

- **Like clouds,** mist is billions of tiny water droplets floating on the air. Fog forms near the ground.

- **Mist forms** when the air cools to the point where the water vapour it contains condenses to water.

- **Meteorologists** define fog as a mist that reduces visibility to less than 1 km.

- **There are four main kinds** of fog: radiation fog, advection fog, frontal fog and upslope fog.

- **Radiation fog** forms on cold, clear, calm nights. The ground loses heat that it absorbed during the day, and so cools the air above.

▲ *Huge amounts of moisture transpire from the leaves of forest trees. It condenses on cool nights to form a thick morning mist.*

- **Advection fog** forms when warm, moist air flows over a cold surface. This cools the air so much that the moisture it contains condenses.

- **Sea fog** is advection fog that forms as warm air flows out over cool coastal waters and lakes.

- **Frontal fog** forms along fronts (see weather fronts).

- **Upslope fog** forms when warm, moist air rises up a mountain and cools.

13

Rain

▲ *Rain starts when moist air is lifted up dramatically. Water drops and ice crystals inside the cloud grow so big that it turns dark.*

- **Rain falls** from clouds filled with large water drops and ice crystals. The thick clouds block out the sunlight.

- **The technical name** for rain is precipitation, which also includes snow, sleet and hail.

- **Drizzle** is 0.2–0.5 mm drops falling from nimbostratus clouds. Rain from nimbostratus is 1–2 mm drops. Drops from thunderclouds can be 5 mm. Snow is ice crystals. Sleet is a mix of rain or snow, or partly melted snow.

14

- **Rain starts** when water drops or ice crystals inside clouds grow too large for the air to support them.

- **Cloud drops grow** when moist air is swept upwards and cools, causing lots of drops to condense. This happens when pockets of warm, rising air form thunderclouds – at weather fronts or when air is forced up over hills.

- **In the tropics** raindrops grow in clouds by colliding with each other. In cool places, they also grow on ice crystals.

- **The world's rainiest place** is Mt Wai-'ale-'ale in Hawaii, where it rains 350 days a year.

  - **The wettest place** is Tutunendo in Colombia, which gets 11,770 mm of rain every year. (London gets about 70 mm.)

Evaporation due to Sun

Air forced to rise

  - **La Réunion in the Indian Ocean** received 1870 mm of rain in one day in 1952.

    - **Guadeloupe in the West Indies** received 38.1 mm of rain in one minute in 1970.

Monsoon reaches land

◀ *Wet air carried by monsoon winds reaches India and Bangladesh where it is forced to rise over hills. As it rises, the air cools and deposits the moisture as rain.*

15

Thunderstorms

▲ *Large, towering cumulonimbus storm clouds can tower up to 16 km in the air.*

- **Thunderstorms** begin when strong updraughts build up towering cumulonimbus clouds.

- **Water drops** and ice crystals in thunderclouds are buffeted together. They become charged with static electricity.

- **Negative charges** sink to the base of a cloud; positive ones rise. When the different charges meet they create lightning.

- **Sheet lightning** is a flash within a cloud. Forked lightning flashes from a cloud to the ground.

- **Forked lightning** begins with a fast, dim flash from a cloud to the ground, called the leader stroke. It prepares the air for a huge, slower return stroke a split second later.

- **Thunder is the sound** of the shock wave as air expands when heated instantly to 25,000°C by the lightning.

- **Sound travels** more slowly than light, so we hear thunder three seconds later for every 1 km between us and the storm.

- **At any moment** there are 2000 thunderstorms around the world, each generating the energy of a hydrogen bomb. Every second, 100 lightning bolts hit the ground.

- **A flash of lightning** is brighter than 10 million 100-watt light bulbs. For a split second it has more power than all the power stations in the USA put together. Lightning travels at up to 100,000 km per second down a path that is the width of a finger but up to 14 km long. Sheet lightning can be 140 km long.

- **Lightning** can fuse sand under the ground into hard strands called fulgurites.

▲ *Few places have more spectacular lightning displays than Nevada, USA. The energy in clouds piled up during hot afternoons is unleashed at night.*

Sunshine

▲ *Without sunshine, the Earth would be cold, dark and dead.*

- **Half of the Earth** is exposed to the Sun at any time. Radiation from the Sun is the Earth's main source of energy. This provides huge amounts of both heat and light, without which there would be no life on Earth.

- **Solar** means anything to do with the Sun.

- **About 41% of solar radiation** is light; 51% is long-wave radiation that our eyes cannot see, such as infrared light. The other 8% is short-wave radiation, such as UV rays.

- **Only 47%** of the solar radiation that strikes the Earth actually reaches the ground; the rest is soaked up or reflected by the atmosphere.

- **The air is not warmed** much by the Sun directly. Instead, it is warmed by heat reflected from the ground.

- **Solar radiation** reaching the ground is called insolation.

- **The amount of heat reaching** the ground depends on the angle of the Sun's rays. The lower the Sun is in the sky, the more its rays are spread out and therefore give off less heat.

- **Insolation is at a peak** in the tropics and during the summer. It is lowest near the Poles and in winter.

- **The tropics** receive almost two and a half times more heat per day than either the North or South Pole.

- **Some surfaces** reflect the Sun's heat and warm the air better than others. The percentage they reflect is called the albedo. Snow and ice have an albedo of 85–95% and so they stay frozen even as they warm the air. Forests have an albedo of 12%, so they soak up a lot of the Sun's heat.

◀ *The Sun can be used to generate electricity. When the sun shines on solar cells, electric current flows from one side of the cell to the other.*

19

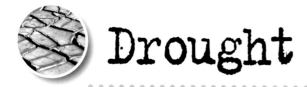

Drought

▲ *In times of drought crops, plants and animals all suffer.*

- **A drought** is a long period when there is too little rain.

- **During a drought** the soil dries out, groundwater sinks, streams stop flowing and plants die.

- **Deserts** suffer from permanent drought. Many tropical places have a seasonal drought, with long dry seasons.

- **Droughts** are often accompanied by high temperatures, which increase water loss through evaporation.

- **Between 1931 and 1938** drought reduced the Great Plains of the USA to a dustbowl, as the soil dried out and turned to dust. Drought came again from 1950 to 1954.

- **Desertification** is the spread of desert conditions into surrounding grassland. It is caused either by climate changes or by pressure from human activities.

- **Drought,** combined with

increased numbers of livestock and people, have put pressure on the Sahel, south of the Sahara in Africa, causing widespread desertification.

- **Drought** has brought repeated famine to the Sahel, especially the Sudan and Ethiopia.

- **Drought** in the Sahel may be partly triggered off by El Niño – a reversal of the ocean currents in the Pacific Ocean, off Peru, which happens every 2–7 years.

- **The Great Drought** of 1276–99 destroyed the cities of the ancient Indian civilizations of southwest USA. It led to the cities being abandoned.

▲ *Drought bakes the soil so hard it shrinks and cracks. It will no longer absorb water even when rain comes.*

21

Cold

▲ *When it is very cold, snow remains loose and powdery and is often whipped up by the wind.*

- **Winter weather is cold** because days are too short to give much heat. The Sun always rakes across the ground at a low angle, spreading out its warmth.

- **The coldest places** in the world are the North and South Poles. Here the Sun shines at a low angle even in summer, and winter nights last almost 24 hrs.

- **The average temperature** at Polus Nedostupnosti (Pole of Cold) in Antarctica is –58°C.

- **The coldest temperature** ever recorded was –89.2°C at Vostok in Antarctica on July 21, 1983.

- **The interiors of the continents** can get very cold in winter because land loses heat rapidly.

- **When air cools** below freezing point (0°C), water vapour in the air may freeze without turning first to dew. It covers the ground with white crystals of ice or frost.

- **Fern frost** is feathery tails of ice that form on cold glass as dew drops freeze bit by bit.

- **Hoar frost** is spiky needles of frost that form when damp air blows over very cold surfaces and freezes onto them.

- **Rime** is a thick coating of ice that forms when drops of water in clouds and fogs stay liquid well below freezing point. The drops freeze hard when they touch a surface.

- **Black ice** forms when rain falls on a very cold road.

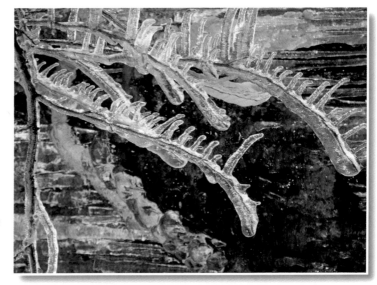

▶ *Rime is a thick coating of ice that forms when moisture cools well below 0°C, before freezing onto surfaces.*

Snow

- **Snow** is crystals of ice. They fall from clouds in cold weather when the air is too cold to melt ice into rain.

- **Outside the tropics** most rain starts to fall as snow but melts on the way down.

- **More snow falls** in the northern USA than falls at the North Pole because it is too cold to snow at the North Pole.

- **The heaviest** snow falls when the air temperature is hovering around freezing.

- **Snow can be hard to forecast** because a rise in temperature of just 1°C or so can turn snow into rain.

- **All snowflakes** have six sides. They usually consist of crystals that are flat plates, but occasionally needles and columns are also found.

▲ *Fresh snow can contain up to 90% air, which is why snow can actually insulate the ground and keep it warm, protecting plants.*

- **W. A. Bentley** was an American farmer who photographed thousands of snowflakes through microscopes. He never found two identical flakes.

- **In February 1959** the Mt Shaska Ski Bowl in California had 4800 mm of snow in just six days.

- **In March 1911** Tamarac in California was buried in 11,460 mm of snow. The Antarctic is buried in over 4000 m of snow.

- **The snowline** is the lowest level on a mountain where snow remains throughout the summer. It is 5000 m in the tropics, 2700 m in the Alps, 600 m in Greenland and at sea level at the Poles.

▶ *Snow is often slow to melt after it has covered the ground. This is because it reflects away the majority of the sunlight.*

Wind

- **Wind is moving air.** Strong winds are fast-moving air; gentle breezes are air that moves slowly.

- **Air moves** because the Sun warms some places more than others, creating differences in air pressure.

- **Warmth makes** air expand and rise, lowering air pressure. Cold makes air heavier, raising pressure.

- **Winds blow** from areas of high pressure to areas of low pressure, which are called lows.

- **The sharper the pressure difference** the stronger the winds blow.

▼ *Energy from the wind is converted to electricity by wind turbines.*

- **In the Northern Hemisphere,** winds spiral in a clockwise direction out of highs, and anticlockwise into lows. In the Southern Hemisphere, the reverse is true.

- **A prevailing wind** is a wind that blows frequently from the same direction. Winds are named by the direction they blow from. For instance a westerly wind blows from the west.

- **In the tropics** the prevailing winds are warm, dry winds. They blow from the northeast and the southeast towards the Equator.

- **In the mid-latitudes** the prevailing winds are warm, moist westerlies.

▲ *The more of the Sun's energy there is in the air, the windier it is. This is why the strongest winds may blow in the warm tropics.*

...FASCINATING FACT...
The world's windiest place is George V in Antarctica, where 320 km/h winds are usual.

27

Tornadoes

- **Tornadoes,** or twisters, are long funnels of violently spiralling winds beneath thunderclouds.

- **Tornadoes** roar past in just a few minutes, but they can cause severe damage.

- **Wind speeds** inside tornadoes are difficult to measure, but they are believed to be over 400 km/h.

- **Tornadoes develop** beneath huge thunderclouds, called supercells, which develop along cold fronts.

- **England** has more tornadoes per square kilometre than any other country, but they are usually mild.

- **Tornado Alley** in Kansas, USA, has 1000 tornadoes a year. Some of them are immensely powerful.

▶ *Tornadoes are especially destructive in central USA but they can occur wherever there are thunderstorms.*

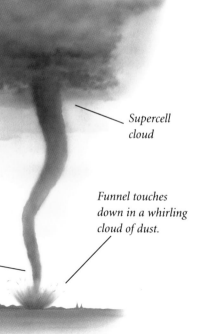

Supercell cloud

Funnel touches down in a whirling cloud of dust.

Cloud base

28

▶ *A tornado starts deep inside a thundercloud, where a column of strongly rising warm air is set spinning by high winds roaring through the cloud's top. As air is sucked into this column, or mesocyclone, it corkscrews down to the ground.*

● **A tornado** may be rated on the Fujita scale, from F0 (gale tornado) to F6 (inconceivable tornado).

● **An F5 tornado** (incredible tornado) can lift a house and carry a bus hundreds of metres.

● **In 1990** a Kansas tornado lifted an 88-car train from the track and then dropped it in piles four cars high.

...FASCINATING FACT...
In 1879, a Kansas tornado tore up an iron bridge and sucked dry the river beneath it.

Hurricanes

- **Hurricanes** are powerful, whirling tropical storms. They are also called willy-willies, cyclones or typhoons.

- **Hurricanes develop** in late summer as clusters of thunderstorms build up over warm seas (at least 27°C).

- **As hurricanes grow,** they tighten into a spiral with a calm ring of low pressure called the 'eye' at the centre.

- **Hurricanes** move westwards at about 20 km/h. They strike east coasts, bringing torrential rain and winds gusting up to 360 km/h.

- **Officially** a hurricane is a storm with winds exceeding 119 km/h.

- Hurricanes last, on average, 3–14 days. They die out as they move towards the Poles into cooler air.

- **Each hurricane** is given a name in alphabetical order each year, from a list issued by the World Meteorological Organization. The first storm of the year might be, for instance, Hurricane Andrew.

▶ *A satellite view of a hurricane approaching Florida, USA. Notice the yellow eye in the centre of the storm.*

▲ *The whirling winds of a hurricane can cause widespread destruction. The storm measures between 320 and 480 km in diameter.*

● **The most fatal cyclone ever** was the one that struck Bangladesh in 1970. It killed 266,000 with the flood from the storm surge – the rapid rise in sea level created as winds drive ocean waters ashore.

● **A hurricane** generates the same energy every second as a small hydrogen bomb.

● **Each year** 35 tropical storms reach hurricane status in the Atlantic Ocean, and 85 around the world.

31

Weather forecasting

- **Weather forecasting** relies partly on powerful computers, which analyse the Earth's atmosphere.

- **One kind of weather prediction** divides the air into parcels. These are stacked in columns above grid points spread throughout the world.

- **There are over one million** grid points. each grid point has a stack of at least 30 parcels above it.

▲ *Meteorologists use information from supercomputers to make weather forecasts for the next 24 hours and for up to a week ahead.*

▶ *This weather map shows isobars – lines of equal air pressure – over North America. It has been compiled from millions of observations.*

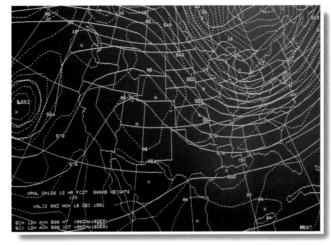

- **At regular intervals** each day, weather observatories take millions of simultaneous measurements of weather conditions

- **Every three hours** 10,000 land-based weather stations record conditions on the ground. Every 12 hours balloons fitted with radiosondes go into the atmosphere to record conditions high up.

- **Satellites in the sky** give an overview of developing weather patterns.

- **Infrared satellite images** show temperatures on the Earth's surface.

- **Cloud motion winds** show the wind speed and wind direction from the way in which the clouds move.

- **Supercomputers** allow the weather to be predicted accurately three days in advance, and for up to 14 days in advance with some confidence.

- **Astrophysicist** Piers Corbyn has developed a forecasting system linked to variations in the Sun's activity.

Weather fronts

- **A weather front** is where a big mass of warm air meets a big mass of cold air.

- **At a warm front,** the mass of warm air is moving faster than the cold air. The warm air slowly rises over the cold air in a wedge. It slopes gently up to 1.5 km over 300 km.

- **At a cold front,** the mass of cold air is moving faster. It undercuts the warm air, forcing it to rise sharply and creating a steeply sloping front. The front climbs to 1.5 km over about 100 km.

- **In the mid-latitudes,** fronts are linked to vast spiralling weather systems called depressions, or lows. These are centred on a region of low pressure where warm, moist air rises. Winds spiral into the low – anticlockwise in the Northern Hemisphere, clockwise in the Southern.

- **Lows start** along the polar front, which stretches round the world. Here, cold air spreading out from the Poles meets warm, moist air moving up from the subtropics.

- **Lows develop** as a kink in the polar front. They then grow bigger as strong winds in the upper air drag them eastwards, bringing rain, snow and blustery winds. A wedge of warm air intrudes into the heart of the low, and the worst weather occurs along the edges of the wedge. One edge is a warm front, the other is a cold front.

- **The warm front arrives first,** heralded by feathery cirrus clouds of ice high in the sky. As the front moves over, the sky fills with slate-grey nimbostratus clouds that bring steady rain. As the warm front passes away, the weather becomes milder and skies may briefly clear.

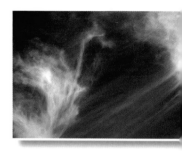

▲ *Feathery cirrus clouds high up in the sky are a clear warning that a warm front is on its way, bringing steady rain. When there is a warm front, a cold front is likely to follow, bringing heavy rain, strong winds and perhaps even a thunderstorm.*

- **After a few hours,** a build-up of thunderclouds and gusty winds warn that the cold front is on its way. When it arrives, the clouds unleash short, heavy showers, and sometimes thunderstorms or even tornadoes.

- **After the cold front passes,** the air grows colder and the sky clears, leaving just a few fluffy cumulus clouds.

- **Meteorologists** think that depressions are linked to strong winds, called jet streams, which circle the Earth high above the polar front. The depression may begin with Rossby waves, which are giant kinks in the jet stream up to 2000 km long.

▼ *This illustration shows two short sections through the cold and warm weather fronts that are linked to depressions in the mid-latitudes.*

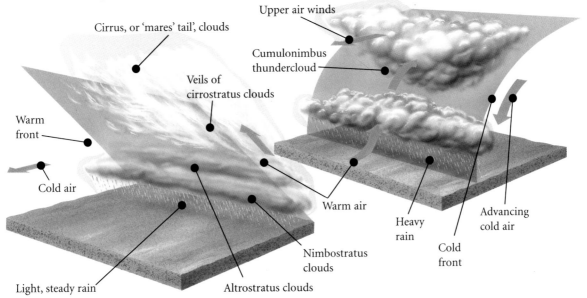

Upper air winds

Cirrus, or 'mares' tail', clouds

Cumulonimbus thundercloud

Veils of cirrostratus clouds

Warm front

Cold air

Warm air

Heavy rain

Advancing cold air

Cold front

Nimbostratus clouds

Light, steady rain

Altrostratus clouds

Air pollution

▲ *Factories pour out a range of fumes that pollute the air.*

- **Air pollution** comes mainly from car, bus and truck exhausts, waste burners, factories, power stations and the burning of oil, coal and gas in homes.

- **Air pollution** can also come from farmers' crop sprays, farm animals, mining and volcanic eruptions.

- **Some pollutants,** such as soot and ash, are solid, but many more pollutants are gases.

- **Air pollution** can spread huge distances. Pesticides, for instance, have been discovered in Antarctica where they have never been used.

- **Most fuels** are chemicals called hydrocarbons. Any hydrocarbons that are left unburned can react in sunlight to form toxic ozone.

▶ *The increased use of cars has made air pollution a serious problem, particularly in the world's largest cities.*

- **When exhaust gases** react in strong sunlight to form ozone, they may create a photochemical smog.

...**FASCINATING FACT**...
Factories in the Chinese city of Benxi make so much smoke the city is invisible to satellites.

- **Air pollution** is probably a major cause of global warming (see global warming).

- **Air pollution** may destroy the ozone layer inside the Earth's atmosphere (see the ozone hole).

- **Breathing the air** in Mexico City is thought to be as harmful as smoking 40 cigarettes a day.

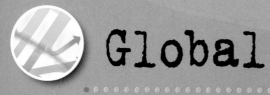

Global warming

▲ *Could global warming make the Mediterranean look like this?*

- **Global warming** is the increase in average temperatures around the world. This increase has been between 0.3°C and 0.8°C over the 20th century.

- **Most scientists** now think that global warming is caused by human activities, which have resulted in an increase in the Earth's natural greenhouse effect.

- **The greenhouse effect** is the way that certain gases in the air – notably carbon dioxide – trap some of the Sun's warmth, like the panes of glass in the walls and roof of a greenhouse.

▶ *The greenhouse effect occurs when carbon dioxide is released into the atmosphere by burning coal and oil (fossil fuels).*

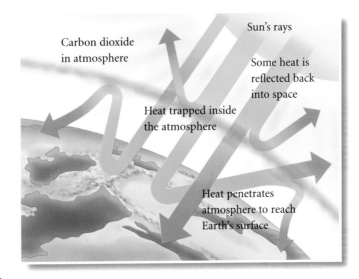

Carbon dioxide in atmosphere

Sun's rays

Some heat is reflected back into space

Heat trapped inside the atmosphere

Heat penetrates atmosphere to reach Earth's surface

- **The greenhouse effect** keeps the Earth pleasantly warm – but if it increases, the Earth may become very hot.

- **Many experts** expect a 4°C rise in average temperatures over the next 100 years.

- **Humans** boost the greenhouse effect by burning fossil fuels, such as coal, oil and natural gas that produce carbon dioxide.

- **Emission of the greenhouse gas** methane from the world's cattle has added to the increase in global warming.

- **Global warming** is bringing stormier weather by trapping more energy inside the atmosphere.

- **Global warming** may melt much of the polar ice caps, flooding low-lying countries such as Bangladesh.

. . . FASCINATING FACT . . .
Recent observations show global warming could be much worse than we thought.

Index